Also Available
from EYE ON EDUCATION

Instructional Leadership for School Improvement
Sally J. Zepeda

The Principal as Instructional Leader:
A Handbook for Supervisors (with CD-ROM)
Sally J. Zepeda

The Call to Teacher Leadership
Zepeda, Mayers, and Benson

Achievement Now!
How to Assure No Child Is Left Behind
Dr. Donald J. Fielder

Navigating Comprehensive School Change:
A Guide for the Perplexed
Chenoweth and Everhart

Data Analysis for Continuous School Improvement,
Second Edition
Victoria L. Bernhardt

The School Portfolio Toolkit: A Planning, Implementation,
and Evaluation Guide for Continuous School Improvement
Victoria L. Bernhardt

Using Data to Improve Student Learning in Elementary Schools
Victoria L. Bernhardt

From Rigorous Standards to Student Achievement:
A Practical Process
Rettig, McCullough, Santos, and Watson

Handbook on Teacher Evaluation:
Assessing and Improving Performance
Stronge and Tucker

Handbook on Educational Specialist Evaluation:
Assessing and Improving Performance
Stronge and Tucker

In appreciation to
Dr. Robert J. Shekletski for his vision and support.

About the Authors

P. Diane Frey, Ph.D., Mary Jane Smart, Ph.D., and Sue Walker all have public school experience, both classroom and administrative, and college level teaching experience in rural, suburban, and urban settings. During their respective careers they provided district-level leadership for programs that gained state and national recognition for excellence.

Their career paths crossed when they worked together over a ten-year period during the 1990s in the School District of Lancaster in Lancaster, Pennsylvania. The School District of Lancaster is a small urban district where a staff of 1000 educates 11,000 racially, culturally, and economically diverse students, including a significant ESL population, in twenty school buildings. During most of the ten-year period they worked together, the District was in the design phase of systemic reform driven by a cutting-edge strategic plan that directed the simultaneous restructuring of the district in the areas of curriculum and assessment, professional development, facilities and technological infrastructure, and governance. The driving force in this transformation was the belief that all children can learn.

The authors were part of a cadre of professionals in the School District of Lancaster Curriculum Office who provided leadership for the design phase of the curriculum, assessment, Early Childhood programming, technology infrastructure, and professional development programming. The resulting design organized the district into instructional levels defined by academic standards and assessments. In recognition of the value of data-driven instructional decisions, technological infrastructure and programming were put in place to improve the monitoring of student progress and establish accountability. Over a five year period, simultaneous with the design work, professional development programming was designed and delivered in the areas of belief, standards, assessments, and technology. The programming served pre-school through high school teachers and included parents and community members. A variety of delivery systems was used, including college courses, district workshops with internal and consultant presenters, and week-long professional centers that included mentoring support in the class-room when new strategies were initially tried.

It is the learning from this exciting work and the acknowledgment of the vital role classroom teachers play in implementing reform that inform this publication.

Table of Contents

Preface

During the 1990s we had a unique opportunity to work together in a school district committed to the systemic reform of teaching, learning, and management. We were part of a professional team who provided leadership for both the design work and the professional development to support implementation. We brought to this work our experience in classroom teaching, administration, college teaching, student teacher supervision, curriculum development, and professional development. Like all who have been privileged to participate in meaningful reform, we were both exhilarated and overwhelmed by the tremendous investment of time, energy, and thoughtfulness the work required. We came to appreciate well the analogy that compares reforming a school district to redesigning an airplane while flying it.

While all of the work was challenging, perhaps the greatest challenge was transforming classrooms to support a diverse student population in achieving the high academic standards that are at the heart of educational reform. We understood that classrooms reflective of research and successful practice looked very different from traditional classrooms. However, user-friendly tools and models that described the transformed classroom were in short supply. A major challenge we faced was helping others visualize a classroom where the successful practice research was translated with automaticity. We found it necessary to access a variety of journals and other publications to create vignettes for professional development purposes.

Like other educators working in reform during that time period, we were influenced by the growing literature and research base on teacher behavior that produced student achievement, including *The National Board for Professional Teaching Standards, Interstate New Teacher Assessment and Support Consortium (INTASC),* and Charlotte Danielson's *Enhancing Professional Practice: A Framework for Teaching.* All of the sources, although driven by somewhat differing purposes, exhibited consistency in the knowledge and behaviors identified to describe the quality of teaching that makes a difference in student achievement. And, all cited a mix of professional consensus, empirical studies, and formal research as the documentation for the knowledge and behaviors identified while acknowledging the critical role that teacher judgment and decision-making play in using the knowledge effectively.

The Standards of Practice in this book are a blend of our combined practical experience in public schools and teacher training institutions with the growing body of literature on quality teaching. We asked ourselves what teacher knowledge and behaviors would support reform initiatives to a higher level on a faster timeline than we experienced in our work. In response, we generated six standards statements: Belief, Communication, Curriculum, Instruction, Assessment, and Professional Development.

We also challenged ourselves to create a user-friendly format for busy educators moving significant educational reform. We focused on a format that can easily be adopted, adapted, or used as a model to create a set of standards unique to a system or building. Toward that end, we defined each standard with a continuum of descriptors that ranges from the graduating teacher education student to the highly skilled professional teacher who positively and significantly influences student achievement. At the end of the Standards section are a series of vignettes to demonstrate practical applications for the continuums.

In closing, we stress the importance of constantly testing these professional practice standards against the evolving research base and successful practice literature on teaching behaviors that influence student achievement. Equally important, we encourage personal reflection on individual classroom practice with a focus on asking questions, collecting data, and changing behavior. Such data-driven decision making is the hallmark of a true profession and a critical element in educational reform.

Standards of Practice
Introduction

That we dramatically ratcheted up our standards for students without in-sisting on commensurate increases in standards for teachers is a chilling in-dictment for all of us: K-12 leaders, policy makers, higher educators, and ad-vocates.

Education Trust. "Not Good Enough:
A Content Analysis of Teacher Licensing
Examinations." *Thinking K-16*, Spring 1999 .

Overview

The school reform debate during the decade leading up to the year 2000 focused heavily on setting academic standards for students and assessing student progress toward meeting those standards. Significant resources were invested in debating who would set the standards, at what levels the standards would be set, in what subjects the standards would be set, how the standards would be measured, and how subjective values would be removed from the standards.

The beginning of the millennium found academic standards for students readily available in all subjects at the national level, in most subjects at the state level, and in a wide range of subjects at the district level. The good news is that most state and district standards are consistent with the national standards. In addition to the standards themselves, a wide variety of assessments are either available or in place at all three levels. These tools have been available to schools and districts since the mid 1990s.

With the standards and assessments in use over a period of years, a disappointing pattern is surfacing. Although some urban schools are seeing gains from students who previously scored in the bottom quartiles, the standards are not driving the predicted—and hoped for—significant gains in achievement by a broad base of students. The emerging thinking is now focused on a missing piece in the standards implementation design. That piece is a set of standards to focus the work of teachers in creating the conditions necessary for all students to experience success in achieving the academic standards. Just as the academic standards establish student accountability, professional practice standards establish teacher accountability.

Professional practice standards have significant implications for individual teachers, for schools and districts, and for preservice teacher training faculties in higher education institutions.

Definition

Teacher quality is the single most important factor in student learning; it is the catalyst that releases the potential of academic standards to improve academic achievement in our nation's schools. Teacher quality is a combination of the knowledge a teacher possesses and a repertoire of assessment and instructional strategies a teacher uses with judgment and professional commitment. There is a critical need for a set of educational standards based on professional consensus and research findings to define effective teaching. These standards specify the quality of teaching needed to ensure that a broad base of students master challenging academic standards.

Standards of Practice define what teachers must know and be able to do to ensure that all students master challenging academic standards.

Uses

The purpose of Standards of Practice is to define the level of teacher quality needed to ensure that all students learn at high levels and therefore experience academic success. Such a tool provides a framework to hire new teachers, define professional growth benchmarks for practicing teachers, and focus professional development for groups of teachers as well as for individual teachers. In addition, it creates a common language for professional dialogues focused on teaching and learning. Schools and districts determine which uses, or combinations of uses, are appropriate to meet agreed-upon goals.

Setting Hiring Criteria for New Teachers

Prior to entering the profession, prospective teachers must attain knowledge of research-based content and pedagogy that prepares them to practice responsibly as the teacher of record for a group of students. Districts are already challenged to retool experienced teachers with newly identified strategies. It is imperative that entering teachers come with a basic knowledge of these strategies and supervised experience in applying them in classroom settings.

While school districts traditionally have not influenced curriculum established by schools of education, the adoption of professional standards of practice for beginning teachers by districts will assist schools of education in defining and establishing curriculum and other experiences for prospective teachers enrolled in their programs. Sharing the criteria with the schools of education, the suppliers of teachers for school districts, requires a response if the schools of education want the districts to hire their graduates.

For example, if districts establish the Novice Level of Standards of Practice proposed in this publication as entry level hiring criteria, then schools of education can use the Novice Level of the standards to define exit criteria for students who aspire to teach. As a result, all course work and field experiences at the college level will focus on student mastery of the standards at the

Novice Level. No student will be recommended for licensure or initial certification who does not meet the standards at the Novice Level.

Defining Professional Growth Benchmarks for Teachers

Standards of Practice provide benchmarks, or continuous improvement performance targets. These targets, as Charlotte Danielson points out in her teaching framework, serve as a road map to guide new teachers and a structure to help experienced teachers become more effective. Many practicing teachers believe they are excellent because in many instances they lack a basis for comparison. Standard descriptors provide snapshots of excellent teaching at various stages of development against which a teacher can measure personal performance. Districts and schools benefit because improved teacher quality increases student success. In addition, quality teachers can be compensated at levels that recognize their excellence.

The Standards of Practice in this publication define four levels of mastery: Novice Level for new teachers entering the teaching profession, Apprentice Level for beginning teachers during their early years in teaching, Professional Level for practicing teachers, and Expert Level for teachers who provide leadership at the school and district levels in addition to teaching at the Professional Level. The distinctions among the levels are in the degree of sophistication teachers exhibit in the application of the knowledge defined by the standard.

The composite of novice descriptors defines the level of acceptable teaching in the classroom on day one of a teaching career. The teacher achieves this level of mastery through studies and field experiences in teacher training programs. The Novice Level teacher should be supported by a mentor who has demonstrated a Professional Level of mastery and who provides feedback and coaching based on classroom observation. The novice immediately begins working to achieve the Apprentice Level and the Professional Level with continuing mentor support. While attaining the Professional Level is dependent on demonstrated mastery and is not time based, the expectation is that the Professional Level will be attained within a period not to exceed five years of teaching. This expectation is based on effective teacher research that shows teachers have both a residual and a cumulative influence on student academic achievement. Both effective and ineffective teachers influence student achievement during the time spent in the classroom with the teacher and continue to influence student achievement for several years after that time. This evidence necessitates removing ineffective teachers from classrooms in a timely manner. While the time frame for achieving the Professional Level of teaching can be debated and modified within reason, the delicate balance between developing effective teachers for the profession and removing ineffective teachers from the profession must remain a primary focus.

The Professional Level of practice defines an effective teacher who deals simultaneously with the complexities of teaching and exhibits flexibility and adaptability in managing the group and teaching the individual. This teacher demonstrates knowledge and strategies basic to broad-based improved student academic achievement and contributes to the profession. The professional teacher moves from depending on mentoring support to participating in collegial support. This level of mastery creates a pool of teachers from which districts and schools select cooperating teachers for student teachers, mentors for novice and apprentice teachers, and leaders for professional development and curriculum development. Professional Level teachers who aspire to and achieve an Expert Level of practice and conduct action research provide a pool from which districts and schools can choose individuals or teams for unique leadership assignments.

Standards of Practice support changes in traditional evaluation and compensation models. Traditional evaluation models assume a beginning teacher, a teacher with five years of experience and a teacher with twenty-five years of experience are equal. Traditional compensation models assume a teacher with twenty-five years of experience is more effective than a teacher with five years of experience. Both assumptions suggest decisions currently being made about the quality of teaching and the level of compensation are not based on data.

Districts can use the Standards of Practice to develop indicators for assessing the work of teachers at their various stages of mastering the complexities of teaching students to higher academic standards. Using the professional standards provides consistent data to measure the quality of teaching, because these standards include descriptors that detail desirable knowledge and behavior and specify performance criteria that define continuous improvement in the knowledge and behavior over time. Teachers know up front the basis for evaluation and administrators have a consistent lens through which to examine teaching.

Districts can also develop a companion instrument to drive differentiated compensation packages based on demonstrated quality of teaching. For example, a teacher in the Apprentice Level who requires a mentor is paid less than a Professional Level teacher who provides and receives collegial support. When differentiated compensation instruments are developed, the pay scale for attaining the Professional Level of the standard should reflect a significant pay increase. Such increases might include movement to a contract extended beyond the traditional school year.

Focusing Professional Development Programming

Long-range and strategic professional development plans and programming can be determined by using the descriptors in the Standards of Practice with the resulting alignment of supervision, evaluation, and professional development. For example, a professional development framework can be developed for each of the levels of performance (apprentice, professional, expert) for all of the standards. These frameworks will be a combination of district-required sessions, district-optional sessions, formal course work, targeted conference programming, mentoring expectations and individually designed options; all of these options must contribute to demonstrated mastery of the criteria for the various stages in the continuum of the standard.

An apprentice teacher who has already demonstrated mastery of the apprentice criteria in assessment can select options in the professional strand; however, most of the emphasis for an Apprentice Level teacher would remain in the apprentice strand. The goal is to demonstrate consistently, in a classroom setting, mastery of the professional level criteria within approximately five years.

The standards are interrelated. A teacher with in-depth knowledge of content needs excellent communication skills and the ability to apply pedagogical knowledge in order to teach students to a high academic standard. Excellence in teaching is a synthesis of knowledge, skills, professional judgment, and commitment.

The vignettes at the end of this book provide examples of how the Standards of Practice can be used to drive professional development.

Standards of Practice

The following Standards of Practice are a synthesis of practical experience and the growing body of literature on quality teaching.

Belief

Teachers develop a vision for their instructional level based on the belief that all students can learn.

Communication

Teachers communicate with students, parents, colleagues, and community to produce learning, inquiry, positive interaction, and collaboration.

Curriculum

Teachers know the content they teach and the research base on how students learn.

Assessment

Teachers know and use formal and informal assessment strategies to monitor, evaluate, and improve student learning and to plan and modify instruction.

Instruction

Teachers design, plan, and implement instruction to ensure that all students achieve academic success.

Professional Development and Responsibility

Teachers critically examine their practice, engage in lifelong learning, and contribute to the enhancement of the profession.

Standards of Practice Format— How to Use This Book

The format of the Standards of Practice contained in this handbook presents a structure for reflecting on teaching and learning and for describing a Professional Level teacher applying the standard in a classroom setting. Each Standard has a Narrative and a Continuum.

The next seven pages display and define a shortened version of the Assessment Standard. The Assessment Standard can be found in its entirety on pages 41 to 48.

Narrative

Standard

Teachers know and use formal and informal assessment strategies to monitor, evaluate, and improve student learning and to plan and modify instruction.

Overview of the Standard

A teacher's knowledge of *asse*[...]ith an understanding of how student[...]dent learning, planning instr[...]educational decision making[...]

Assessment is a continuo[...]learning conditions for stude[...]ment Standard recognizes the[...]that assessment is not a singl[...]mensions of assessment, inc[...]also emphasizes the importanc[...]Through assessment, student learni[...]instruction modified to meet individual student need[...] e of assessment promotes active, inquiry-based learning and accon[...]es individual learning styles and the range of learner needs in the co[...]e, social, emotional, and physical domains of development. The teache[...]s assessment to check continually for understanding, to differentiate b[...]een levels of understanding, and to look at student performance over tim[...]

The assessment standard requires the an[...]lysis of assessment data to provide the basis for improving *content and performance standards* as well as local assessment systems. It also focuses teacher professional development programming and the design of a teacher's personal professional development plan.

> The Narrative consists of the Standard Statement; an Overview of the Standard; Key Vocabulary and Definitions; a description of the Professional Level of Teaching; and Key Concepts contained in that description. The Standard Statement defines the standard. The Overview of the Standard elaborates on the Standard Statement.

Key Vocabulary and Definitions

Assessment

The process of using s̲... tional needs.

Authentic Assessme...

Assessment tasks ...

Content Standards

Statements indicating ... to do.

Performance Standards

Preestablished levels of proficienc... at define mastery of content standards.

Rubric

A scoring guide that differentiates between levels of quality of a product or performance.

Scoring Guide

A resource that contains rubrics, scoring keys, and performance criteria for all activities in a task and may also contain anchor papers to assist in scoring.

The Key Vocabulary and Definitions define critical vocabulary contained in the standard. The vocabulary is highlighted the first time it appears in the text.

Professional Level of Teaching

The teacher meeting the Professional Level of the Assessment Standard demonstrates mastery in the design and use of a variety of assessment strategies to monitor, evaluate, and improve student learning; to plan and modify instruction; and to evaluate and improve academic standards.

Evidence of the knowledge of assessment research is observable in the design and implementation of assessment. In designing assessment to meet academic standards, the teacher id[entifies] ... know and be able to do and the criteria ... dge and performance. The teacher u[nderstands] ... s of different types of assessments an[d] ... s to be used with individual students ...

> The Professional Level of teaching describes the Professional Level teacher applying the standard in the classroom.

In implementing assessments, the te[acher at the Profession]al Level of the Assessment Standard has a wide range o[f asse]ssment strategies and tools to assist students in meeting high academ[ic sta]ndards. Such strategies and tools help teachers get to know individua[l st]udents and how they learn best. The data generated by such strategies are used to guide the next steps in the classroom, thus making assessment an integral part of the daily instructional process. The teacher is able to articulate how assessment has influenced the choice of instructional strategies and how instruction has been modified based on an analysis of assessment data.

In implementing assessments, the teacher communicates the expected goals in advance and provides students with multiple opportunities, contexts, and end products for demonstrating mastery. Students are given appropriate and focused feedback early and often and are provided with opportunities for peer involvement and discussion. The teacher assists students in reflecting on what they have learned and in explaining, interpreting, and applying their knowledge in a variety of real-world situations. The teacher helps students set their own learning goals, monitor their own progress, identify and solve problems that will impede their progress, and assess and improve their own learning. Through the use of assessment, students are able to document, articulate, and communicate their progress. Student self-assessment, reflection, evaluation, and communication are an integral part of the assessment process.

The teacher is also committed to ongoing self-assessment, reflection, evaluation, and professional dialogue and collaboration as a means of improving the assessment process, instruction, and academic standards, and as a tool in designing professional development activities....

Note: This material can be found in its entirety on page 44.

Key Concepts

- The primary purpose of assessment is to improve student learning.
- Assessment is integrated with ins[...]
- Assessment is ongoing.
- Assessment strategies meet indivi[...] and are culturally and socially sensitive.
- Assessment data provides the basis for gui[...]ng educational decision-making and improving academic standards.

Key Concepts highlight critical concepts about the standard.

Continuum

Assessment Standard of Practice

Teachers know and use formal and informal assessment strategies to monitor, evaluate, and improve student learning and to plan and modify instruction.

	Novice: *Emerging Practice*	*Apprentice:* *Developing Practice*
Purpose of Assessment	Teacher uses assessment to check for class and individual understanding of content and to report on student performance.	Teacher uses assessment to monitor student learning and student engagement in order to determine instructional effectiveness.
Assessment Strategies	Teacher uses a variety of formal and informal assessment strategies to monitor and promote student learning.	Teacher assists students in looking critically at their own work, finding ways to improve their work, and in setting personal learning goals.
Assessment Participation	Teacher develops and administers assessment.	Teacher involves students in selecting, creating, and using assessments that are appropriate to the standards and that help students take responsibility for their own learning.
Assessment Data	Teacher uses technology to collect and communicate assessment data to students and parents.	Teacher uses technology to analyze multiple forms of assessment data, to find patterns that can be used to inform practice, and to share assessment results with parents via student-led parent conferences.
Assessment Opportunities	Teacher provides several opportunities during instruction for students to demonstrate learning.	Teacher provides frequent opportunities in multiple formats for students to demonstrate learning.

Professional: Proficient Pratice	Expert: Advanced Practice
Teacher uses assessment to monitor and modify teaching strategies in relation to student achievement.	Teacher uses assessment for schoolwide curriculum improvement and as a means of accountability.
Teacher evaluates his/her use of assessment strategies by monitoring studentachiev	Teacher develops and experiments
Teacher evaluates assess relation to validity, relia bias.	
Teacher uses technology to analyze multiple forms of student data, to formulate questions and inquiry based on that data for action research, and to communicate data to peers, the school, and district for use in the design and improvement of the local assessment system.	Tea technology to ana ultiple forms of stu t and action research to i ove curriculum to set andard, to design state/national assessments and to develop trend lines on student learning.
Teacher provides ongoing opportunities for student involvement in the evaluation of assessments and uses the data gained from this involvement to improveassessments.	Teacher engages peers in ongoing development and evaluation of assessments that will establish a valid and reliable measure of student achievement and growth.

The Continuum defines four levels of professional growth by providing characteristics of excellent teaching at various stages of development. The four levels are: novice, apprentice, professional, and expert.

Belief System
Standard of Practice

"Develop your driving principles and beliefs and base all of your decisions on them. Ruthlessly prune your practices, policies and procedures to remove those that don't support your driving principles."

"Gerry House: Lessons from the Maze" *ASCD Education Update*, January 2002

Belief

Narrative

Standard

Teachers develop a vision for the instructional level based on the belief that all students can learn.

Overview of the Standard

The belief system is the philosophical foundation upon which actions are planned and implemented. A teacher's *belief system*, influenced by classroom experiences both as a student and a teacher, is the lens through which the teacher views and shapes instructional practice. When the individual teacher's beliefs are aligned with the beliefs of the system and of colleagues in a positive way, a maximum amount of time is devoted to planning and delivering instruction that results in high academic achievement.

Teachers who have been successful in reform efforts focused on teaching diverse students to high academic standards share a common belief that all students can learn. Further, they believe that teachers create and control the conditions for success. This belief, focused and unambiguous, shapes the teacher's vision and drives the teacher to define what it is that all students should know and be able to do by the end of the *instructional level*. Finally, the belief translates into classroom practice by significantly influencing a teacher's choice of assessment tasks and instructional strategies that account for *normal patterns of child growth and development*.

This standard acknowledges the instructional level as a structural element embedded in a broader educational continuum. Teachers, driven by belief and vision, *backmap* a plan for the instructional level that integrates instruction and assessment to ensure student success. The resulting plan communicates high expectations for student achievement.

Key Vocabulary and Definitions

Belief System

Philosophical foundation of underlying tenets that are the basis for decisions and actions.

Backmap

A strategy used to determine what students need to know and be able to do by the end of the instructional level and how to organize this information into small segments to be taught throughout the school year.

Instructional Level

The amount of time the system gives a teacher to accomplish specific goals.

Normal Patterns of Child Growth and Development

Patterns that predict how a child's physical, social, emotional, moral and cognitive development, and cultural background affect behavior and learning.

Professional Level of Teaching

The teacher meeting the Professional Level of the Belief Standard demonstrates mastery by communicating high expectations for all students in actions and words. These high expectations are evident in planning, decision making, instructing, and assessing students. The teacher also demonstrates a personal commitment to helping students achieve by creating conditions that encourage students to persist in the face of temporary failure. The teacher does not accept student failure as an option.

The teacher consistently verbalizes for students, parents, and colleagues what students need to know by the end of the instructional level and creates instructional settings to foster success in learning. The teacher continually adds instructional strategies to an existing repertoire and alters assessment formats and instructional settings to meet individual student needs and to capitalize on individual student strengths. In planning instruction, the teacher accommodates the student's physical, social, emotional, moral, and cognitive development and takes advantage of cultural background to introduce new content.

A teacher's belief system is also reflected in student behavior. Students hold themselves to high standards when establishing personal learning goals, which they do consistently as part of the instructional process. Equally important, students persist in seeking academic success.

Key Concepts
- All students can learn at high levels.
- Teachers create and control conditions for success.
- High expectations for student learning are initially set by the teacher.
- Students learn to set high self-expectations.

Continuum

Belief System Standard of Practice

Teachers develop a vision for their instructional level based on the belief that all students can learn.

	Novice: Emerging Practice	Apprentice: Developing Practice	Professional: Proficient Practice	Expert: Advanced Practice
Expecta-tions	Teacher believes that all children can learn and sets high expectations for student achievement.	Teacher sets expectations for students and backmaps those expectations based on what students need to know and be able to do by the end of the instructional level.	Teacher expects students to establish high self-expectations when setting personal learning goals.	Teacher trains staff in the use of district support systems that help children meet expectations.
Practices	Teacher uses a limited repertoire of instructional strategies.	Teacher uses an expanded number of instructional strategies and persists in seeking alternative strategies.	Teacher creates conditions and provides strategies to support students in successfully taking responsibility for their own learning.	Teacher designs and validates new strategies based on beliefs about classroom practices that result in improved student achievement.

Communication Standard of Practice

> *Research shows, however, that teachers are the single most trusted communicators about education issues, particularly through their one-on-one interactions with parents.*
>
> Panasonic Foundation, Inc.
> "Turn on the Power—Communi-
> cate!" *Panasonic Partnership Program,*
> Spring 1996

Narrative

Standard

Teachers communicate with students, parents, colleagues, and community to produce learning, inquiry, positive interaction, and collaboration.

Overview of Standard

A teacher's *communication skills* directly influence student learning and parent and community perception and support of district and school learning goals. The Communication Standard recognizes the direct relationship between effective *communication strategies* and quality education.

Because teachers far outnumber other system employees and have daily contact with students, they are the key communicators of school and district messages to students, parents, colleagues, and community members. This combination of numbers and direct access ensures that the influence of teacher communicators far outweighs the influence of any other communicator in the district. This influence plays out in student learning and in community support of schools.

Proficient communication is dependent on mastery of skills and strategies basic to communicating clearly in written and oral modes with a variety of audiences. These skills and strategies include knowledge of cultural influences and body language as well as knowledge of strategies for writing, active listening, questioning, providing feedback, and summarizing.

School reform requires very different methods of teaching, learning, assessing, and communicating. The accomplished teacher is able to communicate constructive feedback to students, parents, and colleagues about what students have learned and concise information about school and district goals and priorities. The teacher as the key communicator of school and district messages plays a critical role in achieving parent and community support of reform.

Key Vocabulary and Definitions

Communication skills

Technical knowledge base of the conventions of standard English language in reading, writing, speaking, and listening.

Communication strategies

Techniques basic to successful interaction with diverse individuals and groups of individuals.

Professional Level of Teaching

The teacher meeting the Professional Level of the Communication Standard demonstrates mastery by communicating in both oral and written modes to effect desired changes in understanding, interaction, and action whether the audience is students, parents, community members, or colleagues.

In both speaking and writing for the purpose of providing information to the target audience, the teacher uses clear, concise, and accurate language with vocabulary that is audience appropriate. The use of techniques to engage the target audience, such as incorporating interests of individuals in the audience into the presentation, is observable. The teacher responds to individuals in the audience with relevant feedback that demonstrates cultural sensitivity and understanding of verbal and nonverbal language. The teacher consistently achieves positive engagement with the audience, understanding by the audience, and desired action from the audience. The successful communicator also achieves interaction among the audience members: parents discussing with parents, students working with students, and colleagues dialoging with colleagues. When communicating with an audience whose first language is not English, the teacher uses strategies such as controlled vocabulary to enhance communication given in the English language. When appropriate, the teacher secures a translator for audiences whose first language is not English.

The communication knowledge base at the Professional Level translates into observable activities. In community and parent forums, student-led conferences to review academic progress with parents occur along with student demonstrations of new instructional techniques. Positive action agendas result from interaction among participants at community forums. In addition, parents and teachers use electronic means to communicate regularly about student academic performance and attendance. In the classroom, small group learning activities are observable. The teacher communicates regularly with individual students about interests and academics and often combines the two topics. Conversations about student learning occur among teachers during planning time. All of these activities occur because a teacher understands and uses communication skills and strategies to effect desired understanding, action, and interaction.

A Professional Level knowledge base of the Communication Standard empowers a teacher to be a successful facilitator in any school related setting—the classroom, community forums, parent conferences, meetings, and collegial and professional development sessions.

Key Concepts

- A teacher's skill in communication directly influences student learning.
- The teacher is the key communicator of school and district messages to parents and community members.
- Teacher communication is critical to sustaining school reform.

Continuum

Communication Standard of Practice

Teachers communicate with students, parents, colleagues and community to produce learning, inquiry, positive interaction, and collaboration.

	Novice: Emerging Practice	*Apprentice: Developing Practice*
Communication Skills and Strategies	Teacher communicates clearly and accurately in writing and orally, using conventions of standard English and verbal and nonverbal techniques.	Teacher listens actively and responds thoughtfully, using technology and other supports to enhance communication.
Communication with Students	Teacher uses questioning and discussion techniques to present information and assignments to students.	Teacher modifies communication based on cultural sensitivity and verbal and nonverbal feedback.
Communication with Parents about Student Progress	Teacher communicates formally at scheduled times using district/school formats and informally as needed.	Teacher maintains ongoing communication with families to exchange information about student progress, including student-led conferences.
Communication with Parents about School Priorities	Teacher presents prepared information to parents and responds to questions.	Teacher prepares and presents information to parents and responds to questions.
Communication with Community	Teacher presents prepared information about the state of the school to target audience and responds to questions.	Teacher prepares and presents information about the state of the school to target audience and responds to questions.

Professional: Proficient Practice	Expert: Advanced Practice
Teacher knows the process of second language acquisition and uses strategies to support learning of students whose first language is not English.	Teacher designs district level communications in a variety of formats and for a range of audiences.
Teacher consistently achieves student engagement and understanding through effective use of a variety of communication strategies.	Teacher trains colleagues in culturally sensitive communication strategies and techniques to engage students.
Teacher involves students in communication with families through student-led demonstrations and performances.	Teacher trains colleagues in interactive parent communication techniques.
Teacher demonstrates school programs and learning priorities and achieves parent understanding.	Teacher achieves parent support of school programs and learning priorities.
Teacher facilitates target audience discussion of planned changes, summarizes points of agreement and disagreement, and identifies next steps.	Teacher achieves target audience support of planned changes.

Curriculum
Standard of Practice

The content that students are taught influences the level of student achievement.

> James A. Banks et al. "Diversity within Unity: Essential Principles for Teaching and Learning in a Multicultural Society," *Phi Delta Kappan*, November 2001

Narrative

Standard

Teachers know the content they teach and the research base on how students learn.

Overview of Standard

A teacher's *content knowledge* in a *discipline*, combined with an understanding of how students learn, directly influences student achievement. The Curriculum Standard recognizes that relationship by specifying an in-depth knowledge of both discipline content and learning theory.

Knowledge of content includes facts, concepts, principles, structures, relationships, issues, assumptions, and methods of inquiry central to the discipline. This knowledge requires the ability to demonstrate. For example, a language arts teacher can write a narrative that meets set standards, and a science teacher can design and conduct science experiments. In addition, content knowledge includes recognition that the knowledge base is not fixed but evolving. Finally, this teacher knowledge encompasses the critical understanding of common student misconceptions related to the discipline and how to use the misconceptions to teach accurate concepts.

Knowledge of learning theory included in the Curriculum Standard focuses on the underlying research base of how children learn. This base consists of *child development theory* and *multiple intelligences theory*. A teacher well grounded in this knowledge understands what students bring to the educational setting developmentally, experientially, and culturally, and knows that individual variation within the theoretical predictors is expected and does occur. The teacher incorporates the diversity of the experiences within the classroom into the learning process. The applications of learning theory, the instructional strategies, are addressed within the Instruction Standard.

The Curriculum Standard acknowledges differences between generalists, such as elementary teachers, and specialists, such as secondary subject teachers, in the area of content knowledge. However, the standard for the generalist is raised to ensure enriched content teaching for all students.

Key Vocabulary and Definitions

Content Knowledge

Facts, concepts, principles, structures, relationships, assumptions, issues, and methods of inquiry central to a discipline.

Discipline

A field of study, such as mathematics.

Child Development Theory

A theory that predicts how a child's physical, social, emotional, moral and cognitive development, and cultural background affect behavior and learning.

Multiple Intelligences Theory

A theory that predicts intelligence is multifaceted, that it is fluid, and that vigorous learning changes the physiology of the brain.

Professional Level of Teaching

The teacher meeting the Professional Level of the Curriculum Standard demonstrates mastery in the design and implementation of instruction as well as in professional development participation.

In designing a standards-based curriculum, the teacher identifies central organizing concepts within the disciplines and uses the concepts to create interdisciplinary learning experiences that require students to integrate knowledge, skills, and methods of inquiry from several disciplines. The learning experiences connect to real world settings. Encouragement for students to examine, question, and interpret ideas from diverse perspectives is evident in teacher use of centric interpretations, differing and often contradictory viewpoints, and varying methods of inquiry. The curriculum design accommodates the range of learner needs in the cognitive, social, emotional, and physical domains of development by providing multiple contexts for learning reflective of the cultural groups within the classroom and by encouraging a variety of end products as evidence of student mastery of the academic standards.

This knowledge base is also observable in curriculum implementation through the methods teachers use to manage and facilitate the work of students. Students use primary and secondary sources in a variety of formats; textbooks are one of many resources they access. Students also test hypotheses using the methods of inquiry and standards of evidence used in the discipline by artists and scholars. Teachers use multiple representations and explanations of concepts to highlight key ideas and link new knowledge to prior student knowledge; teachers incorporate cultural influences in assessing prior student knowledge. They continually identify student misconceptions and use the misconceptions to teach accurate concepts. Finally, teachers consistently access their in-depth content knowledge and understanding of learning theory to make the adjustments necessary to meet individual needs of students.

A keystone component of the professional development plan that a Professional Level teacher designs is an investment in keeping the knowledge of discipline content and learning theory current.

Key Concepts

- A teacher's knowledge of content directly influences student achievement.
- Content is interrelated.
- Content knowledge has organizing structures unique to the various disciplines.
- Knowledge of and access to a variety of resources is basic to understanding content.
- Student learning is informed by theory based on research.

Continuum

Curriculum Standard of Practice

Teachers know the content they teach and the research base on how students learn.

	Novice: Emerging Practice	Apprentice: Developing Practice
Content Knowledge	Teacher knows content of disciplines taught as defined in district/state/national standards for the level taught and for one level above and below.	Teacher articulates the content students should know by the end of the level taught.
Structure of Knowledge	Teacher knows how content knowledge in the discipline is organized	Teacher knows the work of key scholars and artists in the discipline.
Linkage to Other Disciplines	Teacher connects central organizing concepts within each discipline.	Teacher connects central organizing concepts between and among disciplines.
Selection of Resources	Teacher selects textbooks for scope, content, accuracy, and currency using written criteria and compensates for omissions, errors, and outdated information.	Teacher selects supplemental resources, including technology, to enrich, extend, and update textbooks.
Child Development Theory	Teacher knows the physical, social, emotional, moral, and cognitive characteristics of students as they progress through developmental stages and understands the impact of culture on behavior and learning.	Teacher knows the theory of multiple intelligences.

Professional: Proficient Practice	Expert: Advanced Practice
Teacher knows common student misconceptions and how to use these misconceptions to teach accurate content.	Teacher conducts research to create content knowledge.
Teacher knows the modes of critical thinking necessary to analyze content knowledge.	Teacher uses appropriate research methodology to create content knowledge.
Teacher connects content to real-world settings and problems.	Teacher projects influence of new knowledge on disciplines.
Teacher selects primary and secondy sources in a variety of formats to replace textbooks as the dominant resource.	Teacher produces resources to meet the unique needs of the discipline.
Teacher knows that multiple contexts improve academic achievement among diverse student populations.	Teacher knows the most recent brain research and reflects on the implications for teaching and learning.

Assessment
Standard of Practice

Multidimensional assessment taps the power and diversity of active learning, creates multiple sources of information to support instructional decision making, and helps students become more reflective and capable learners.

> M. Kulieki et al. *Why Should Assessment Be Based on a Vision of Learning?* NCREL, Oak Brook, 1990

Narrative

Standard

Teachers know and use formal and informal assessment strategies to monitor, evaluate, and improve student learning and to plan and modify instruction.

Overview of the Standard

A teacher's knowledge of *assessment* and instruction, combined with an understanding of how students learn, is a powerful tool for improving student learning, planning instruction, raising academic standards, and guiding educational decision making.

Assessment is a continuous, ongoing process designed to create the best learning conditions for students and ensure academic success. The Assessment Standard recognizes the rapidly expanding research base emphasizing that assessment is not a single event and promoting multiple forms and dimensions of assessment, including *authentic assessment*. The research base also emphasizes the importance of integrating assessment into instruction. Through assessment, student learning is continually monitored and instruction modified to meet individual student needs. The use of assessment promotes active, inquiry-based learning and accommodates individual learning styles and the range of learner needs in the cognitive, social, emotional, and physical domains of development. The teacher uses assessment to check continually for understanding, to differentiate between levels of understanding, and to look at student performance over time.

The assessment standard requires the analysis of assessment data to provide the basis for improving *content and performance standards* as well as local assessment systems. It also focuses teacher professional development programming and the design of a teacher's personal professional development plan.

Key Vocabulary and Definitions

Assessment

The process of using student performance to determine instructional needs.

Authentic Assessment

Assessment tasks that have a "real life" context.

Content Standards

Statements indicating what students should know and be able to do.

Performance Standards

Preestablished levels of proficiency to define mastery of content standards.

Rubric

A scoring guide that differentiates between levels of quality of a product or performance.

Scoring Guide

A resource that contains rubrics, scoring keys, and performance criteria for all activities in a task and may also contain anchor papers to assist in scoring.

Professional Level of Teaching

The teacher meeting the Professional Level of the Assessment Standard demonstrates mastery in the design and use of a variety of assessment strategies to monitor, evaluate, and improve student learning; to plan and modify instruction; and to evaluate and improve academic standards.

Evidence of the knowledge of assessment research is observable in the design and implementation of assessment. In designing assessment to meet academic standards, the teacher identifies what the student should know and be able to do and the criteria that will be used to judge that knowledge and performance. The teacher understands and articulates the purposes of different types of assessments and the appropriate assessment strategies to be used with individual students and the content being assessed.

In implementing assessments, the teacher meeting the Professional Level of the Assessment Standard has a wide range of assessment strategies and tools to assist students in meeting high academic standards. Such strategies and tools help teachers get to know individual students and how they learn best. The data generated by such strategies are used to guide the next steps in the classroom, thus making assessment an integral part of the daily instructional process. The teacher is able to articulate how assessment has influenced the choice of instructional strategies and how instruction has been modified based on an analysis of assessment data.

In implementing assessments, the teacher communicates in advance the expected goals and provides students with multiple opportunities, contexts, and end products for demonstrating mastery. Students are given appropriate and focused feedback early and often and are provided with opportunities for peer involvement and discussion. The teacher assists students in reflecting on what they have learned and in explaining, interpreting, and applying their knowledge in a variety of real-world situations. The teacher helps students set their own learning goals, monitor their own progress, identify and solve problems that will impede their progress, and assess and improve their own learning. Through the use of assessment, students are able to document, articulate, and communicate their progress. Student self-assessment, reflection, evaluation, and communication are an integral part of the assessment process.

The teacher is also committed to ongoing self-assessment, reflection, evaluation, and professional dialogue and collaboration as a means of improving the assessment process, instruction, and academic standards, and as a tool in designing professional development activities.

Rubrics and scoring guides are used to judge student performance. The teacher continually clarifies the criteria used for judging student performance, supported by the best current understanding of the discipline. Performance criteria help the teacher determine what a good performance looks like, i.e., one that meets the standard, and define what is valued in student work. Performance criteria also help students know what is expected of them, know when they are successful, and make decisions about the quality of their own work. Such criteria help teachers and students define and clarify content and performance standards and help provide a common vocabulary for discussing student work in relation to the standards. Rubrics clearly communicate what constitutes excellence and are a powerful motivational tool for students that help them continually work toward higher levels of quality.

Scoring guides require teachers continuously to clarify, refine, and revise the criteria for evaluating student work. Through the use of scoring guides, teachers provide better student feedback that relates specifically to the task and to the standards. Examples of student work illustrating the various criteria help to provide more precise definitions and help in applying the scoring criteria uniformly to each performance.

In a standards-based system, levels of performance are used to measure student progress against the standards. Grading and reporting are criterion-referenced. Performance on each standard is reported for each student.

Key Concepts

- The primary purpose of assessment is to improve student learning.
- Assessment is integrated with instruction.
- Assessment is ongoing.
- Assessment strategies meet individual student needs and are culturally and socially sensitive.
- Assessment data provides the basis for guiding educational decision-making and improving academic standards.

Continuum

Assessment Standard of Practice

Teachers know and use formal and informal assessment strategies to monitor, evaluate, and improve student learning and to plan and modify instruction.

	Novice: Emerging Practice	*Apprentice: Developing Practice*
Purpose of Assessment	Teacher uses assessment to check for class and individual understanding of content and to report on student performance.	Teacher uses assessment to monitor student learning and student engagement in order to determine instructional effectiveness.
Assessment Strategies	Teacher uses a variety of formal and informal assessment strategies to monitor and promote student learning.	Teacher assists students in looking critically at their own work, finding ways to improve their work and in setting personal learning goals.
Assessment Participation	Teacher develops and administers assessments.	Teacher involves students in selecting, creating, and using assessments that are appropriate to the standards and that help students take responsibility for their own learning.
Assessment Data	Teacher uses technology to collect and communicate assessment data to students and parents.	Teacher uses technology to analyze multiple forms of assessment data, to find patterns that can be used to inform practice, and to share assessment results with parents via student-led parent conferences.
Assessment Opportunities	Teacher provides several opportunities during instruction for students to demonstrate learning.	Teacher provides frequent opportunities in multiple formats for students to demonstrate learning.

Professional: *Proficient Practice*	Expert: *Advanced Practice*
Teacher uses assessment to monitor and modify teaching strategies in relation to student achievement.	Teacher uses assessment for schoolwide curriculum improvement and as a means of accountability.
Teacher evaluates his/her use of assessment strategies by monitoring student achievement.	Teacher develops and experiments with alternative assessments and shares results with the larger learning community.
Teacher evaluates assessments in relation to validity, reliability, and bias.	Teacher involves peers and the larger community in critically evaluating assessments and assessment strategies.
Teacher uses technology to analyze multiple forms of student data, to formulate questions and inquiry based on that data for action research, and to communicate data to peers, the school and district for use in the design and improvement of the local assessment system.	Teacher uses technology to analyze multiple forms of student and action research data to improve curriculum, to set standards, to design state/national assessments, and to develop trend lines on student learning.
Teacher provides ongoing opportunities for student involvement in the evaluation of assessments and uses the data gained from this involvement to improve assessments.	Teacher engages peers in ongoing development and evaluation of assessments that will establish a valid and reliable measure of student achievement and growth.

Instruction
Standard of Practice

Sustaining research-based instructional strategies in the classroom is an arduous process that calls for commitment at every level.

"Honing the Tools of Instruction:
How Research Can Improve
Teaching for the 21st Century."
ASCD Curriculum Update,
Winter 2002

Narrative

Standard

Teachers design, plan, and implement instruction to ensure that all students achieve academic success.

Overview of the Standard

Effective instruction, instruction resulting in academic achievement by a broad base of diverse students, is a blending of wisdom about teaching, learning, students, and content knowledge. Such instruction is dependent on planning, design, and implementation within a climate of organization and support that produces a culture that fosters learning. If students do not learn, instruction is ineffective. The focus of this standard is the consistent use of research-based strategies to plan and deliver instruction within such a culture.

Classroom organization and management include strategies teachers use to create an optimal learning environment in the instructional setting so that the time and focus are spent on productive learning. Classrooms where students achieve are disciplined learning environments that reflect some common elements. Teachers establish norms, roles and responsibilities for interaction in the classroom and arrange the area physically to support instruction. They recognize the importance of peers in establishing an optimal learning environment and involve students in establishing guidelines and parameters for classroom behavior. Teachers use their knowledge of human behavior to promote self-motivation in students and instill a sense of self-discipline and persistence basic to becoming independent learners who assume responsibility for their own learning. Classroom organization and management strategies directly influence the success of instruction.

Planning is the pre-instructional thinking and design work teachers complete individually and in teams for the purpose of identifying and elaborating curricular goals, developing activities, selecting strategies, defining assessments, and collecting materials and resources. The resulting written plans, long- and short-term, are based on *preassessments* and other student input and connect students with their current understanding to the new content knowledge to be mastered. In designing the plans, teachers select teaching and learning strategies and materials that will blend curricular goals and meet student needs. The plans are interdisciplinary requiring students to apply skills and use methods of inquiry from several content areas. Teachers understand that all plans require continuous adjustment based on student feedback and student work.

Implementation includes the challenge of instructing the group while differentiating to meet individual needs. Instructing requires a specific knowledge of how to convey subject matter to students and persistence in doing so. During instruction, teachers function in different roles including instructor, facilitator, coach, and audience. The role selected is driven by the content and by student needs. A common element in all roles is teaching students to pose and solve problems. Teachers know when and how to adjust approaches based on monitoring student *engagement* and student progress.

Implementing the instructional plan includes preassessing students to form initial *flexible groups* and ongoing formal and informal assessments to regroup students frequently based on instructional strengths and needs. *Differentiation* is the modification or modifications teachers make to individualize instruction for students or small groups of students with the ultimate goal of academic success for all. Teachers differentiate content, activities, assessment products, and learning environments and do so by creating multiple contexts, pathways, and forms of assessment. Differentiation is dependent on the range of strategies a teacher can access and the teacher's understanding of the advantages and limitations of the strategies. An integral part of differentiation is determining when and what outside resources are appropriate to support exceptionalities and other student needs and strengths.

Professional Level of Teaching

The teacher meeting the Professional Level of the Instruction Standard of Practice demonstrates mastery on a daily basis in the classroom in managing, planning, and teaching.

In managing, the teacher helps students work cooperatively in groups and work productively as individuals. Planned transitions between and within activities are evident to optimize use of instructional time. The physical setup of the instructional area reflects the content being taught and the strategies being used. The teacher is consistent in reinforcing positive behavior and in responding to misdirected behavior. Students set high expectations for themselves and demonstrate pride in the work they produce.

In planning, the teacher creates learning experiences to make content meaningful to students and consciously selects strategies that support both content and student needs. Student contributions to the planning are evident in the classroom activities. Resources available in the classroom reflect the teacher's planned accommodation of both exceptionalities and second language acquisition. The teacher continuously adjusts pacing of instruction and modifies instructional plans based on student feedback and student work.

In teaching, the teacher makes conscious decisions about roles to play and strategies to use by frequently sampling student thinking either orally or in writing. A pattern of student engagement in learning is evident in group work and individual work. Active learning is the norm in the classroom where students search for patterns, pose problems, and seek solutions. Question-generated discussions are frequent where thoughtful questions are posed and all students respond and participate in the resulting discussions. The teacher adjusts instruction based on student responses by adding activities, elaborating on content, altering activities, and working with small groups and individuals. Perhaps most obvious is a constant monitoring for student comprehension and responding to misconceptions.

The teacher individualizes instruction based on student needs and strengths by differentiating the instructional setting, the instructional activities, and the assessment products. Grouping is always flexible and changes often to meet the needs of students. Informal and formal assessment provides student feedback that informs the differentiation. Specialists and volunteers are evident in the classroom to meet specific needs identified by the teacher.

The teacher who meets the Professional Level of the Instruction Standard assesses groups and individuals, creates plans leading to the next level of development and achievement, and continuously modifies the plans during implementation to capitalize on student strengths as a basis for growth and student errors as an opportunity for learning.

Key Concepts

- Classroom organization and management influence academic achievement.
- Instructional plans are based on knowledge of content, students, and strategies.
- Instructional plan adjustments are based on student feedback and student work.
- Effective teachers make conscious decisions about teaching strategies based on a knowledge of the strategies and their strengths and limitations in relation to student needs.
- Differentiation is a critical factor in broad-based academic achievement.

Continuum

Instruction Standard of Practice

Teachers design, plan, and implement instruction to ensure that all students achieve academic success.

	Novice: Emerging Practice	*Apprentice: Developing Practice*
Classroom Organization and Management	Teacher creates a learning environment to support positive social interaction and active engagement in learning by managing student behavior and classroom procedures and by organizing physical space.	Teacher involves students in establishing parameters for social interactions among students and between students and teacher and in assuming responsibility for classroom interactions.
Planning	Teacher, as an individual and a team member, applies the basic elements of instructional design to produce coherent, written instructional plans for standards-based learning that are content-appropriate and student-relevant and provide for exceptionalities.	Teacher integrates content standards from various disciplines and connects new learning to students' prior experiences and current learning.
Delivery of Instruction	Teacher provides individual, whole group, and small group instruction based on an understanding of the child development research base.	Teacher monitors instruction for full student engagement and adjusts and differentiates instruction based on formal and informal assessment data.
Differentia- tion	Teacher uses a range of strategies, including technology, to customize instruction based on student data.	Teacher continuously forms flexible groups based on formal and informal assessments and adjusts instruction to meet group needs.

Professional: Proficient Practice	Expert: Advanced Practice
Teacher motivates students to show persistence during temporary failure and promotes self-motivation and self-discipline in students.	Teacher provides professional development focusing on strategies that create an instructional setting where students learn and achieve.
Teacher motivates students to assume responsibility for shaping their instructional tasks.	Teacher produces district level, coherent, written instructional plans for adaptation or adoption by teams of teachers in the system.
Teacher models, coaches, and facilitates self-directed learning by engaging students in posing problems and working through alternative solutions.	Teacher validates the impact of instructional strategies on student achievement through action research.
Teacher creates multiple contexts and pathways and uses multiple forms of assessment to individualize instruction based on student data.	Teacher provides professional development on differentiation strategies.

Professional Development and Responsibility Standard of Practice

There is growing evidence that student performance is influenced by high-quality preservice education and by professional development opportunities for on-the-job teachers.

Linda Darling-Hammond. "Target Time Toward Teachers." *Journal of Staff Development*, Spring 1999

Narrative

Standard

Teachers critically examine their practice, engage in lifelong learning, and contribute to the enhancement of the profession.

Overview of the Standard

Professional development is a critical component of improved student learning. The Professional Development and Responsibility Standard of Practice recognizes that relationship by requiring teachers to examine critically their practice, engage in lifelong learning, and contribute to the profession.

In critically examining their practice, teachers continually review student achievement data to inform educational decision making. They reflect on the teaching and learning that have occurred, review the teaching strategies that were used, determine the success and/or failure of student learning, and evaluate their performance as teachers. Professional development opportunities are used to study and reflect on research, define and solve problems, and improve academic standards, instructional strategies, and assessments.

Engaging in lifelong learning requires teachers to keep their knowledge of discipline content and learning theory current, expand their repertoire of instructional and assessment strategies, engage in *action research*, adapt their teaching to new research findings, and develop new approaches to organizing and managing their classrooms and schools.

The Professional Development and Responsibility Standard recognizes the importance of contributing to the profession by encouraging teachers to become members of learning communities; to share their knowledge, skills, and results of action research with the larger professional community; and to engage in professional discourse on improving practice.

The Professional Development and Responsibility Standard fosters the norm of continuous improvement extending throughout a teacher's career. Teachers develop personal professional improvement plans that are closely linked to school initiatives on improving practice and student achievement.

These plans are embedded in the teachers' work and are grounded in research. The success of professional development is linked to high and challenging content and performance standards and improved student achievement.

Key Vocabulary

Professional Development

An ongoing process of professional growth designed to improve practice and student achievement.

Action research

Disciplined inquiry using the techniques of research in which teachers formulate questions about current practice, engage in experimentation, collect and analyze data and use the results to improve practice.

Professional Level of Teaching

The teacher meeting the Professional Level of the Professional Development and Responsibility Standard engages in action research in content, instructional strategies, and assessment. The teacher is committed to reflection and evaluation and actively seeks out and participates in professional networks and learning communities. Such a teacher is able to formulate a personal professional development plan that informs practice and leads to professional growth and improvement.

In engaging in action research, the teacher formulates questions and inquiry based on knowledge of discipline content, continuous self-assessment and reflection, evaluation of practice, and analysis of multiple forms of student data. The teacher experiments with instructional strategies, tests new theories, collects and analyzes data, and adapts teaching and learning to new research findings. Action research supports teachers in becoming data driven decision makers.

The teacher meeting the Professional Level of the Professional Development and Responsibility Standard of Practice engages in self-reflection following all instructional and assessment activities. The teacher reflects on the engagement of students, the quality of the resulting student work, whether the approach was appropriate and worked well, whether the lesson achieved its goals, and whether students achieved success. This reflection helps the teacher to refine and improve practice.

The teacher participates in professional networks and learning communities by mentoring novice teachers, sharing knowledge and skills with others, presenting workshops and demonstrations, engaging in peer observation and assessment, collaborating with other professionals, engaging in professional dialogue, and examining research. All of these activities have the goals of improving practice, communicating excellence, and improving student achievement.

The teacher meeting the Professional Level of the Professional Development and Responsibility Standard of Practice determines the content and format of a carefully designed personal professional development plan that is based on research and analysis of student data and indicates how the implementation of the plan will result in changes in classroom practice, improvement of instruction, and student success. It provides for ongoing assessment of professional growth.

Key Concepts

- Professional development is critical to improved teacher practice that results in higher student achievement.
- Professional development is ongoing.
- The success of professional development is measured by student achievement.

Continuum

Professional Development and Responsibility

Teachers critically examine their practice, engage in lifelong learning, and contribute to the enhancement of the profession.

	Novice: *Emerging Practice*	*Apprentice:* *Developing Practice*
Content Knowledge	Teacher uses professional development to deepen and enhance content knowledge.	Teacher uses professional development to build a content research base that translates into practice.
Tools, Strategies, Processes	Teacher uses professional development opportunities to acquire assessment and instructional strategies that are responsive to the developmental needs of students, to acquire technological proficiency, and to understand and use data to improve student performance.	Teacher uses professional development opportunities to develop assessment and instructional strategies that are research based and standards driven, to learn how to integrate technology into all aspects of their work, and to analyze data to improve student performance.
Collaboration	Teacher participates on teams as a means of professional development.	Teacher participates in collegial groups to share expertise and resources and to engage in professional discourse for classroom improvement.
Professionalism	Teacher participates in mentoring program and designs professional development activities to facilitate growth toward a particular goal.	Teacher participates in mentoring program and engages in self-assessment and reflection to achieve professional development goals.

Professional: *Proficient Practice*	Expert: *Advanced Practice*
Teacher uses professional development to define problems and formulate questions about the content and engage in action research.	Teacher uses professional development to contribute to the profession's content knowledge base by leading professional development activities and sharing results of action research.
Teacher uses professional development opportunities to analyze current practice, to organize and analyze results of action research, to create and evaluate new instructional strategies developed through data analysis, and to use technology in organizing and analyzing data.	Teacher uses professional development opportunities to share new assessment and instructional strategies with other teachers, to share technological applications and proficiency, and to facilitate discussions of school and classoom-based data.
Teacher participates in professional networks to share expertise and resources and to engage in professional discourse for school improvement.	Teacher leads professional networks and learning communities and assumes a leadership role in the school and district.
Teacher mentors others and is committed to personal professional development as an ongoing process based on a vision of teaching and learning.	Teacher recognizes a professional responsibility for leading others in developing and continually refining appropriate practice, engaging in life-long learning and modeling the highest professional standards.

Standards in Action:
Novice Teacher

Principal

Dr. Williams has been meeting with each of the teachers in his building for their annual review. His next appointment is with Lyn Martin who has just completed her first year in Lakeview School District.

Dr. Williams knows that Lyn graduated from State University and that her class is the first to benefit from the collaboration between the district and the university. The Lakeview administrative team has been meeting regularly with State University representatives to share their expectations for beginning teachers. Lakeview School District is working diligently to create schools in which all of the students and staff are learning and performing at high levels and the district/university partnership and collaboration have helped.

As Dr. Williams reviews Lyn's file and reflects on her work this past year, he begins to make notes for his meeting with her. Since Lyn is a relatively new teacher, Dr. Williams knows that his role and the primary purpose of this meeting is to provide a focus for her work next year and to provide guidance on how to involve her mentor and other colleagues in her work. Collegial support is critical in helping teachers grow professionally and Lakeview School District encourages it.

The formal evaluations completed by him and by the content supervisor are also in Lyn's file. Dr. Williams takes a few minutes to review each of these and notes the recommendations contained in each.

Finally, Dr. Williams reviews the staff development options that are available this summer through the district, the university, and the local consortium. He knows the district options were developed after careful analysis of student performance data and staff needs and were designed to have sustained impact on teacher knowledge, classroom practice, and student learning. He makes a note of those that might be helpful to Lyn based on the information he has just reviewed.

During the annual review meetings, Dr. Williams focuses teachers on defining where they are in their professional practice. Lakeview School District has developed a continuum for professional practice and has set the expectation that teachers will reach the Professional Level within five years. Although the five year time frame is not an absolute and can be modified, the administrative team and Board of Directors of the Lakeview School District recognize the influence that teacher quality has on student achievement and want teachers to achieve the Professional Level in a timely manner. Dr. Williams uses the annual review meetings as an opportunity to discuss with teachers what it will take to move them to the next level on the continuum. Lakeview School District has tied its compensation package to teacher improvement, so this discussion is an important one.

As Dr. Williams completes his reflection and review of Lyn's work, he thinks about the building and district goals, the professional development options available, and he notes the following points for discussion when he meets with Lyn:

- Increase depth of knowledge of curriculum and content resources.
- Become more data-driven in practice. Begin to analyze multiple forms of student data to improve instructional effectiveness.
- Increase repertoire of instructional strategies.
- Involve students in learning and assessment. Note: A study group might help here.
- Improve communication.
- Review district professional practice continuum. Discuss goals and time line.

Following the annual review meeting, Dr. Williams provides teachers with an opportunity to assimilate the discussion and then asks them to complete a professional development plan that reflects that discussion. This plan will guide their work during the next school year. When teachers complete their plan and bring it to him for review, Dr. Williams requires teachers to be able to articulate how the implementation of their plan will result in changes in their classroom practice, improvement of instruction, and student success.

Teacher

Lyn Martin has just completed her first year at Lakeview School District. She is preparing her professional development plan to discuss with her principal following her annual review meeting with him. She realizes that for the most part, she has been well prepared by State University for teaching. She credits that, in part, to the communication and collaboration she knows have been taking place between the school district and State University. She knows that Lakeview School District has been communicating the expectations they have for first-year teachers to State University. Her class was the first to benefit from this collaboration. Lyn is also expected to provide feedback to State University about this collaboration.

Lyn has participated in the district's new teacher induction program this year and has had a mentor working with her throughout the year. The mentor has observed her class on occasions when she has been a bit frustrated and needed direction. The discussions they've had following those observations proved very beneficial and have helped Lyn to assess and improve her instructional strategies. Her mentor has also helped her to analyze student data to evaluate the effectiveness of her instruction.

The seminars she has attended as part of the induction process and the required reflection component have helped her with classroom organization and management, planning, and parent communication and involvement. These seminars also continually reinforced the belief that all children can learn and the need to set high expectations for student achievement. The collegial group discussions that have taken place during the induction seminars have made her realize the importance of these beliefs and expectations and have provided ideas and strategies to translate these beliefs in her classroom.

As Lyn reflects over the past year and the various induction experiences, she begins to assess her own strengths and weaknesses. She feels confident in her classroom organization and management techniques, but realizes she still needs to improve her communication with parents, perhaps to start involving students in those communications. She also understands the need to differentiate instruction and increase her repertoire of instructional strategies.

Lyn reviews the results of her observations this year. She realizes the recommendations fall into four main areas:

- *Curriculum*

  Increase your depth of knowledge of the content and its inter-relatedness. Spend some time reviewing the content above and below the level you teach. Move away from reliance on the textbook. Begin to incorporate other resources.

- *Assessment*

  Continue to review student data as a key to your instructional effectiveness. Offer more opportunities for students to demonstrate their learning more often. Provide more opportunities for students to assess their own learning.

- *Instruction*

  Use more small-group instruction as a way of better meeting student needs. Use preassessing as a way of grouping students for instruction.

- *Communication*

  Try to incorporate more questioning and discussion techniques as a way of involving students in instruction. Begin to explore other ways to involve students. Improve communication with parents. Provide more support to those students whose first language is not English.

As a first-year teacher, Lyn realizes she has much to learn, but is pleased that the district provides opportunities for teachers to grow professionally. The district provides mentors for teachers beyond the first year, provides opportunities for teachers to observe expert teachers in the district and elsewhere, and encourages teachers to participate on teams. The district also encourages participation in professional organizations and provides incentives for teachers to engage in professional development opportunities that will help them become more proficient in their practice.

Based on the information she has collected through her experiences with her mentor, from observing other teachers, the recommendations from her principal and content supervisor, and her own reflections, Lyn develops her professional development plan for the next school year.

Professional Development Plan

Lyn Martin, Lakeview School District

Standard	Target Indicator
Curriculum	Increase content knowledge to communicate central organizing concepts to students as an integral part of instruction.
	Lessen dependence on textbooks by using multiple resources, including technology, with increasing frequency.

Action	Documentation
Review with mentor, central organizing concepts for level taught and one level above and below.	Develop succinct content statements to communicate to students what current instruction is contributing to content expectations for the instructional level.
Observe mentor and other professional or expert level teachers with focus on how they frame and articulate content expectations for students during instruction.	Classroom observations will confirm that consistent clear articulation of content expectations is an integral part of instruction.
Attend district workshop focused on using content standards to plan instruction.	Written instructional plans will note use of content materials, and strategies from workshops.
Join district middle level content study group that meets monthly to discuss content standards and related instructional strategies.	Written instructional plans will reflect instructional strategies discussed and Professional Portfolio journal will include reflection on strategies used, noting influence on student achievement.
Plan with the school library media specialist and use the district online resource bank to convert a text-based instructional sequence to a multi-resource base.	Lesson plans will reflect multi-resource base for a unit.
Implement instructional sequence with mentor support.	Professional Portfolio journal will include reflection on effectiveness of approach in terms of student work and student interest.

Standard	Target Indicator
Communication	Increase student involvement in instruction by consistently checking for student engagement and understanding during instruction.
	Increase communication with parents by contacting each parent a minimum of once per marking period.
	Provide more support for students whose first language is not English by using controlled vocabulary with ESL students.

Action	Documentation
Attend district workshops on questioning techniques and Socratic Seminars.	Professional Portfolio will include workshop materials and notes in Professional Development section.
Observe mentor and other Professional/Expert level teachers with focus on techniques used to engage students in instruction.	
Team teach with mentor, practicing techniques.	Professional Portfolio journal will include reflection on value of techniques used and mentor feedback.
Work with library media specialist to set up e-mail exchange with parents.	Professional Portfolio will include number of parents who accessed the messages and their perceived value by parents.
Work with mentor to develop a series of messages that are focused on student achievement and can be personalized.	
Attend district workshop on differentiation strategies recommended for ESL students and target strategies for feedback from mentor and supervisor.	
Observe ESL teachers using controlled vocabulary.	Classroom observations will document consistent use of controlled vocabulary with ESL students.

Standard	Target Indicator
Assessment	Review and analyze student data to increase instructional effectiveness.
	Provide more opportunities for students to demonstrate their learning more often and more opportunities for students to assess their own learning.
	Demonstrate a greater depth of understanding of assessment and its role in improving instructional and student achievement.

Action	Documentation
Review and analyze student data from ongoing classroom assessments, from state assessments, and from standardized tests. Identify strategies that will address weak or deficient areas as indicated in Instructional Action Plan.	Professional Portfolio will include the following documentation: analysis of student data from four sources, changes in instructional strategies resulting from analysis, improvement in student performance as measured by local assessments after changes in instructional strategies.
Observe an Expert teacher. Note the frequency of assessments, how the teacher involved students in designing assessments and in providing alternative assessments, how the teacher monitored student work and progress, and how students/peers were involved in assessing progress.	Professional Portfolio will include a summary of the observation focused on the items listed in the action step with reflection on how the information gathered impacted classroom practice.
Ask mentor to observe class and provide feedback on assessment strategies and student involvement.	Professional Portfolio will document feedback from mentor and a reflection on how the feedback influenced classroom practice.
Join a building assessment study group.	Professional Portfolio journal will include sessions attended and written summary of strategy discussions. A personal reflection will identify which strategies have been used in the classroom and the influence noted on student engagement and performance.

Standard	Target Indicator
Instruction	Increase student engagement.
	Use data to group students.

Action	Documentation
Attend workshops and conferences focused on instructional strategies to increase student engagement.	Professional Portfolio will include a list of workshops and conferences attended.
Observe an expert teacher using instructional strategies that fully engage students in instruction.	Professional Portfolio will include written documentation of the observation focused on strategies that engage students.
Plan and team teach with an expert teacher who uses strategies that engage students.	Professional Portfolio will include the plan used and reflection completed after team teaching.
Use strategies that engage students in the classroom setting.	Classroom observations will confirm that students are fully engaged.
Conference with expert teacher to use data to form initial groups.	Professional Portfolio will include written documentation of how data influenced student grouping.
Meet with expert teacher to review student data as a basis for regrouping students.	Professional Portfolio includes reflection on relationship between grouping and student achievement.

Standards in Action: Apprentice Teacher

Principal

Dr. Williams has been meeting with each of the teachers in his building for their annual review. His next appointment is with Deb Smith, a third year teacher in the Lakeview School District. He received Deb's professional portfolio last week and has reviewed it thoroughly.

As Dr. Williams examines Deb's file and reflects on her work this past year, he begins to make notes for his meeting with her. He knows that Deb has set a personal goal of achieving the Professional Level by the end of next school year, so he notes that this should be part of his conversation with her. Deb is currently functioning at the apprentice level but has demonstrated mastery at the Professional Level in some areas.

The formal evaluations completed by him and by the content supervisor are also in Deb's file. Dr. Williams takes a few minutes to study each of these and notes the recommendations contained in each. He also reviews the notes he made as he examined her professional portfolio.

Finally, Dr. Williams reviews the staff development options that are available this summer through the district, the university, and the local consortium. He knows the district options were developed after careful analysis of student performance data and staff needs and were designed to have sustained impact on teacher knowledge, classroom practice, and student learning. Based on the information he has just reviewed, he makes a note of those that might be helpful to Deb.

During the annual review meetings, Dr. Williams focuses teachers on defining where they are in their professional practice, using their Professional Portfolio to document growth. Lakeview School District has developed a continuum for professional practice and has set the expectation that teachers will reach the Professional Level within five years. Although the five year time frame is not an absolute and can be modified, the administrative team and Board of Directors of the Lakeview School District recognize the influence that teacher quality has on student achievement and as such want teachers to achieve excellence in a timely manner. Dr. Williams uses the annual review meetings as an opportunity to discuss with teachers what it will take to move them to the next level on the continuum. Lakeview School District has tied its compensation package to teacher improvement, so this discussion is an important one.

As Dr. Williams completes his reflection and review of Deb's work, he begins to think about where Deb is on the various continuums of professional practice. His assessment of Deb's work indicates that she has demonstrated mastery of the content. Deb has taken workshops, joined study groups and professional organizations, observed expert teachers, and team taught with expert teachers. However, his assessment is that she is still experiencing difficulty with automaticity, i.e., knowing how to deliver the content consistently and appropriately for each student. This level of delivery that is automatic, consistent, and appropriate is what Deb Smith still needs to work on and, once mastered, will take her to the next level on the continuums of professional practice.

Keeping in mind this assessment, the building and district goals and initiatives, and the staff development options available, he makes note of the following points for discussion when he meets with Deb.

- Consistently use primary and secondary resources in a variety of formats to replace textbooks as dominant resources.
- Increase effectiveness of communication with ESL students to improve academic achievement.
- Begin to involve peers and others in critically evaluating assessments and assessment strategies.
- Involve students in looking at data to support individual student needs and in developing individual learning plans based on that data.
- Formulate questions and inquiry and conduct action research.

Each teacher is required to document growth and achievement of goals through the use of a Professional Portfolio. The Professional Portfolio is examined and discussed at the annual review meeting. Following the annual review meeting, Dr. Williams provides teachers with an opportunity to assimilate the discussion and then asks them to complete a professional development plan that reflects that discussion. This plan will guide their work during the next school year. When teachers complete their plan and bring it to him for review, Dr. Williams requires teachers to be able to articulate how the implementation of their plan will result in changes in their classroom practice, improvement of instruction, and student success.

Teacher

Deb Smith is a third-year teacher in the Lakeview School District. She is currently functioning at the Apprentice Level but has demonstrated mastery at the Professional Level in some areas. It is the end of the school year and she is preparing to meet with her principal to discuss her professional development plan for next year.

As Deb prepares for her meeting with the principal, she reviews the data she has collected about her performance this year. Deb begins by reviewing the recommendations from the observations she has had this year. Recommendations from those observations include:

- Identify more primary and secondary resources in a variety of formats.
- Involve students in looking at data to support individual student needs.
- Involve students in developing individual learning plans based on data.
- Formulate questions and inquiry and conduct action research.
- Improve communication with students whose first language is not English with focus on improving academic achievement.
- Begin to involve peers and others in critically evaluating assessments and assessment strategies.

During their annual meeting, the principal complimented her on the manner in which she has communicated with parents this year and the way she has involved students in that communication. She has been able to achieve greater parent understanding, consensus, and support of school and district priorities. She also has done a good job of communicating assessment data to parents, colleagues, the school, and district.

The principal also complimented her on the variety of communication strategies she has used with students. However, she is still experiencing some difficulties in reaching those students whose first language is not English. She has used multimedia presentations and other support to enhance communication, but formal and informal assessment data indicate she is not reaching all of these students effectively.

Deb also has a mentor who has worked with her throughout the school year. With the help of her mentor, Deb used assessment data to monitor and change her teaching strategies and to involve students in assessment, including the evaluation of assessment strategies. She has done a good job of keeping students actively engaged in learning and focused on instructional goals, of involving them in peer and self-assessment, and in providing multiple contexts for students to demonstrate their learning. She continually evaluates her own assessment strategies. However, she has not yet involved students in looking at data to help determine their needs and developing plans for meeting those needs.

As Deb continues her reflection, she realizes she still has many questions in her own mind about district standards. She feels comfortable with the standards and feels she has mastered most of them. The challenge for her, as she sees it, is integrating the standards effectively in the classroom to achieve higher levels of student learning. She also needs to work on creating alternative assessments that meet the standards and locating primary and secondary resources in a variety of formats that support the standards. She knows that some of these concerns can be answered through her professional networks and study groups and professional dialogue with colleagues, but she also realizes that some of the concerns she has can only be answered by experimentation and the analysis of resulting data. She recognizes the need to become involved in action research. Deb uses the data she has collected to create her professional development plan.

Professional Development Plan

Deborah Smith

Standard	Target Indicator
Curriculum	Consistently use primary and secondary resources in a variety of formats to replace textbooks as dominant resources.
Communication	Increase effectiveness of communication with ESL students to improve academic achievement.
Assessment	Begin to involve peers and others in critically evaluating assessments and assessment strategies.

Action	Documentation
Use district resource bank and work with mentor, librarian, and department supervisor to convert remaining text-based instructional sequences to a multi-resource base that includes a mix of primary and secondary sources.	Written instructional plans will reflect conversion to multi-resource base. Classroom observations will confirm consistent use of a variety of secondary and primary resources.
Complete an intensive weekend course at the university on second language acquisition research and supporting strategies.	Professional Portfolio will include transcript in Professional Development section.
Plan a series of instructional sequences with ESL Professional Level teacher and team teach sequences with Professional Level ESL teacher.	ESL mentor feedback on team taught lessons will be included in Professional Portfolio.
Incorporate strategies in written instructional plans.	Professional Portfolio will include academic profile of ESL students in class.
Involve assessment study group in reviewing assessments and assessment strategies and identifying those areas that need improvement. Discuss how these practices might be improved.	Professional Portfolio journal will include a reflection on how assessment practices have changed or improved as a result of working with assessment study group and provide examples of "before" and "after" assessment practices.

Standard	Target Indicator
Instruction	Involve students in looking at data to support individual student needs.
	Involve students in developing individual learning plans based on data.
Professional Development	Formulate questions and inquiry and conduct action research.

Action	Documentation
Observe an Expert Level teacher involving students as they look at data to meet individual needs.	Professional Portfolio will include a reflection from the observation focused on how students look at data to meet individual student needs. Specific steps on how students are taught to look at data will be included.
Team teach with an Expert Level teacher who has students looking at data.	Professional Portfolio will include a reflection of team teaching with an Expert Level teacher as students look at data. Specific steps used by the Expert teacher will be included.
Incorporate strategies that teach students to look at data to meet individual needs.	
Use data with students to develop student's learning plans.	
Students will chart and analyze data and develop student's learning plans based on this data.	Professional Portfolio includes strategies students used to analyze data.
	Teacher observations will document that student's learning plans are developed and implemented using appropriate data.
	Professional Portfolio will include examples of the charted and analyzed data accompanied by the student's learning plans.
Review multiple forms of student data, district content standards, instructional goals, and results of integration efforts. Share data with Expert Level teacher and together formulate questions, design study, and implement.	Share design of study and findings with professional network. Discuss how the findings impact practice. Include a copy of the design of the study and the findings in Professional Portfolio.

References

Association for Supervision and Curriculum Development (2002). "Gerry House: Lessons from the Maze." *Education Update,* no. 1, January, 44, 1–2.

Association for Supervision and Curriculum Development (2002). "Honing the tools of instruction." *Curriculum Update,* Winter: 2.

Banks, James A. et al. (2001). "Diversity within unity: Essential principles for teaching and learning in a multicultural society." *Phi Delta Kappan,* no. 3, November, 83, 198.

Danielson, Charlotte. (1996). *Enhancing professional practice: A framework for teaching.* Arlington, VA: Association for Supervision and Curriculum Development.

Darling-Hammond, Linda. (1999) "Target time toward teachers." *Journal of Staff Development,* no. 2, Spring, 20, 32.

Education Trust. (1992). "Not good enough: A content analysis of teacher licensing examinations." *Thinking K–16,* no.1, Spring, 3, 2.

Interstate New Teacher Assessment and Support Consortium. (1992). *Model Standards for Beginning Teacher Licensing and Development: A Resource for State Dialogue.* Washington, DC: Council of Chief State School Officers.

Kulieki, M. et al. (1990). *Why Should Assessment Be Based on a Vision of Learning?* Naperville, IL: North Central Regional Education Laboratory, p. 6.

National Board for Professional Teacher Standards. (1989). *What teachers should know and be able to do.* Arlington, VA: National Board for Professional Teacher Standards.

Panasonic Foundation, Inc. (1996) "Turn on the Power—Communicate!" *Panasonic Partnership Program,* no. 3, Spring, 5, 2.

Standards
of Practice for
Teachers:

A **ok**

EYE ON EDUCATION
6 DEPOT WAY WEST, SUITE 106
LARCHMONT, NY 10538
(914) 833–0551
(914) 833–0761 fax
www.eyeoneducation.com

Library of Congress Cataloging-in-Publication Data

Frey, P. Diane.
    Standards of practice for teachers : a brief handbook / P. Diane Frey, Mary Jane Smart, Sue A. Walker.
        p. cm.
    Includes bibliographical references and index.
    ISBN 1-930556-73-X
    1. Teachers--Rating of--Handbooks, manuals, etc. 3. Education--Standards--Handbooks, manuals, etc. I. Smart, Mary Jane. II. Walker, Sue A. III. Title.

LB1728.F74 2004
371.14'1--dc22

2003064216

10 9 8 7 6 5 4 3 2 1

Editorial and production services provided by
Richard H. Adin Freelance Editorial Services
52 Oakwood Blvd., Poughkeepsie, NY 12603-4112
(914-471-3566)

Index